Ode to MOTHERHOOD

Ode to MOTHERHOOD

Poems *for* My Mothers

FRANKLIN W. DOUGLAS

ODE TO MOTHERHOOD
POEMS FOR MY MOTHERS

iUniverse books may be ordered through booksellers or by contacting:

iUniverse
1663 Liberty Drive
Bloomington, IN 47403
www.iuniverse.com
1-800-Authors (1-800-288-4677)

ISBN: 978-1-5320-5493-8 (sc)
ISBN: 978-1-5320-5494-5 (e)

Library of Congress Control Number: 2018908925

Print information available on the last page.

iUniverse rev. date: 08/16/2018

To My Siblings,

Who understand the words I wrote
And are cognizant of our ancestral path,
Inspire and empower me to pay homage
To the lives and memories of motherhood—
Through drench and dreg, blood and death,
Instill in us the characters of life
That shaped the destiny of this generation!

To My Daughter,

Encased in these warm lines of mine
Are my victories and my disappointments;
My pain, my anguish, and my excitement;
Good feelings and moody ones;
My dreams, my thoughts, and my doubts;
My pleasure mixed with some despair;
My delight—creative, artistic, and otherwise.
Everything I pass unto you and more
In an enduring love that gives to restore.
It is my joy to watch you take charge and compete.
Still, it's not full if being full means being complete,
For there it is, transcending to my granddaughter.

CONTENTS

PREFACE

Ode to Motherhood

An anthology of contemporary poems
Written partly in free verse,
Short stories in the form of memoirs
Of my personal experiences and more,
Celebrating the lives of all mothers
And the mothers who raised me.

Forty-five autonomous pieces
Pay homage to the mothers of the world
Who endured to lift their children up,
Regardless of the obstacles they faced,
And found ways around and gave their all,
Selflessly and unconditionally.

Mothers are the cradle of humanity,
The triune of humility,
The virtues of fecundity,
The origin of modern thoughts
Where ancient thoughts give rise
To the divinity of motherhood.

Mothers are the progenitors of songs and prayers
And bring harmony the physical way,
Whose impacts outlive their physical stay
And stay around as long as breath endures,
Shaping new hearts and souls
From the very hearts they bear.

Mothers are the procreators of motherhood.
Their existence equates oxygen in living cells.
If their physical existences are now memories,
Let's immortalize them by sharing their memoirs.
I celebrate mine by sharing these poems.
So let's all celebrate motherhood!

Inspiration: A Personal Reflection

On the third day of March 1992, Mama died. She took her last breath at 9:14 p.m., and I was not there. I was caged in a hospital nestled in the sheltered encampment on the Mona campus of the University of the West Indies.

It was a quarantined enclosure with a stainless steel frame and double-paned glass doors. There was no window, and the door could be opened only from the outside. There was an exhaust vent in the upper left corner of the room, with a fan that provided ventilation. I spent many sleepless hours staring at it, wondering where the exhausted air went. Did it pass through a fumigation chamber and recycle? I never figured out that mystery.

A telephone sat on the desk for external communication. This was maximum security at its best, but it was within the confines of these cell walls that I found the remainder of myself ... I did not sleep that night. I could not. I was in too much pain to sleep or focus on anything. Bugzy, a close friend of mine, was the last person I saw that night. He helped me lie down in a comfortable position before he left, but that comfort lasted for only so long. The night was loaded with nightmarish, hellish moments, and I wished I could really find comfort in death, but my mind was far too active and refused to let me go.

Strange as it might sound, the distance and places my mind traveled while I was left balancing on the brink of time, life, and death created the inspiration for my formal writing, a tribute to the mothers who raised me. Being left out there on the brink of time clarified the congestion, and I knew then exactly where I was going.

The very spot and position in which Nettie, my sister-in-law, found me at 6:14 a.m. that Friday morning was the same spot and position I had been lying in since 9:14 p.m. Thursday night. She came in through the cell door to tell me that Mama had died and that she could get me to a place where someone could provide the answers I sought. Little did she know that I had sought and found the answers while balancing on the very brink of life.

I asked her to help me to a sitting position. I then asked her when and at what time Mama had died. The cloud began to compress around me, aspirating and suffocating me. I then said to her in an imposing tone, "I am all right. Could you leave me alone?"

She tried to utter something else, and I looked at her. My expression must have been intense, because the words froze in her throat and she immediately exited through the cell door.

My siblings and I were all products of her old rugged frame. All this flooded my thoughts as tears streamed down my cheeks. As I reminisced on the mothers who'd raised me, I—in poetic arrangements—configured and transformed their lives from temporal into a mythical reality, exposing the naked truth, the purity of the goddess in them.

One of the first poems I wrote for this collection was "The Transfiguration." As I looked at my mother in the casket, I did not recognize what my eyes beheld, and I knew she had slipped away because she was not there. Her body bore no resemblance of the woman with whom I had lived and known all my life. I cried not because she was gone but because I did not know where she had gone.

A feeling of abandonment, loss, and total emptiness welled up inside me. I knew she would not have left without telling me where to find her. Tears rolled down my cheeks, and Sister Nin, my eldest sister, came over with a white handkerchief and wiped them from my face. I looked at her, and my tears stopped. Mama had wiped the tears from my eyes and had whispered in my ear, "It's all right. I am here." Suddenly it was so profoundly peaceful that a smile broke across my face.

The night before my brother Ronnie died, I knew something dreadful was going to happen, but the vision I got focused on Sister Nin. When I looked at Ronnie lying in state in the church, I could not control myself. My emotion let loose, my mind tightened, and I could not breathe. The emptiness, that same feeling, crept up inside me. It was like double jeopardy.

I found myself walking out of the church and up to Sister Nin's house. I held her in my arms and sobbed. Then I bawled like a baby. She looked into my eyes, wiped the tears from my face with a white handkerchief, and whispered in my ear, "It's all right. I am here." A sense of peace overshadowed me, and the tears stopped. I walked back to the church and directed the flow of curious onlookers.

ACKNOWLEDGMENTS

I wish to thank William Raymond, who provided such profound inspiration for the nucleus of my writing and who taught me a lesson or two on judgment. Thanks for being there when I was so vulnerable in my embryonic stage.

I also wish to thank Marlene McPherson for collecting the bits and pieces of my scattered thoughts and collating them into *Ode to Motherhood*.

CHAPTER 1

WHO IS A MOTHER?

Figure of a Mother Holding a Child (*Lupingu lwa Cibola*), nineteenth century. This Congolese figure of motherhood is believed to offer protection through the intervention of spirits by the Bwanga Bwa Cibola society for mothers who experienced emotional trauma from the loss of successive children through miscarriages or infant deaths, Brooklyn Museum photograph.

Mothers of the World

Mothers of the world, the cradle of humanity.
Mothers are my sisters, the vines of fecundity.
Mothers are of all times, the triune of reality,
The trinity in unity, the conception of personalities,
Manifest the actualization in beauty and purity.
Mothers are the antecessors, the origin of thoughts,
Where ancient thoughts give birth to free will
For the good of all will that is good.

Mothers are the progenitors who bring harmony
And healing into physical reality
And give the world songs—and those who sing,
Who endure long-suffering as long as breath lasts,
From whom we all rise and climb the mountain peak
And soar like eagles with open talons and beaks.
Then they secede before we have time to retreat
But leave us alone to be on our own
With the mantle to seek and speak.

Selflessness

Conceived from a crater of curious innocence,
Mama dug and burrowed out a life from Rhoda.
She molded it into personalities of more than ten
And to each infused her character in a unique pen,
Bestowed what she must, installed all she had,
And gave everything, and nothing she ever retained
So that we might write our own story unfeigned.

Mama never lived the rose garden adorned
But slept on ivory made of hidden thorns.
Pain she knew well, and pain she endured,
And when you or I cried was when she cried,
Achingly but painlessly; selflessly she bore it all,
Saddled with our burdens as if we were spineless dolls.

From Berry Hill, Newport, in Manchester
To rocky Blackwoods in red Clarendon,
For her that's where it all registered,
The first of fourteen surviving kindred
To become the matriarch not by choice
But by giving her all and taking none.

A biological father she never had,
But Simeon gave her a name and all she needed
And, like the geometric pattern of creation,
Subdivided one sphere into fourteen separate lives.
But still she retained the image untarnished and genuine.
All this she poured into her siblings, barring none
So they too could give into life abundantly more.

To her grandchildren she made no exception.
For each she gallantly returned to motherhood,
Carving existence sometimes from nothing,
And where she glimpsed a chance of hope,
She delegated adoption not only to rescue
This generation from failing but also to live to give.

The House That Mama Built

My brother never forgave my father
For leaving him in a dungeon of despair,
Abandoned in the custody of my mother,
With no life skill and adulthood filling the air.
He despised her for a role she couldn't fill
And loathed her, using the only weapon
In his arsenal that could break her will.
He tried to stop her from building us a squat
On the only plot of land my father had bought
From the sale of a cow that he had helped to tend,
Now the only hope of rescuing us in the end.

The house where we were all born
And lived our formative lives tumbled down,
And we were engrossed in sheltered life
At my eldest sister's husband's house,
But he had other kids older than his wife
Who were not pleased at sharing their bones.
They too resented and carried the grudge
For a made-up family that was not their own,
So they made living there an uncomfortable hell.

My mother decided to get us out of there
Even if we had to sleep in the open air,
But for us she wouldn't take the chance,
For fear we would catch the deadly cold.
So she dropped her pride and counted the advance,
Stuck away over the years, now priceless gold.
She took the loot to Brother Canute the builder
And mounted her acquaintance call,
And everyone chipped in and did a part
To build a house of refuge as a symbol to all,
Except my brother, who pledged to tear it apart.

Nobody had money to contribute.
What they had was their labor only,
Which they all threw in with no grouse
To excavate the clay and silt to build a house,
To break the stones at nights
Under the watchful eyes of bottle torches,
To mix the mortar in the daylight.
Rough hands shoveled with tender touches,
Laid the ground for a three-bedroom block,
And laced the corners with the blood of the cock
To erect the house that Mama built.

So began the house at the foot of Shop Hill,
Built by the strength of her will with no bill.
We laid the foundation with unity, poured after the drill
Rolled the rocks too heavy to lift down Shop Hill
Carried them inside hampers hung from the jenny's sack
Then sledged them into bits
So the mortar could fit,
Carried water from the cistern
One bucket at a time,
Balanced on our heads,
Rushed to and fro.

Standing on top of Shop Hill,
Is like time standing still—
A lonely structure warmly embraced
Mixed in the canopy with reluctant grace.
Then the zinc roof was sprung
And doors and windows hung.
Two bedrooms were a livable pad,
So we moved in all we ever had,
Our bodies included in the quilt,
Into the house that Mama built.

We didn't sleep in the open air
And we didn't catch the cold,
But my brother moved in
And shared the room with us.
That was where he got married
And where his nine kids were born,
In the house that Mama built.

She Washed My Feet

I sat silently remorseful, humbled by her grace.
With awe in my thoughts, I looked upon her placid face
As she washed the dirt from my feet to soothe my calluses,
My parched and baked feet, ashen with sea salt
Like the salted codfish from New Brunswick
That gave up their lives so we could live.

Like a wavering flame refusing to extinguish,
Smothered in liquid wax, a burning wick
Alight although the wax already melted,
My bruised and scaled feet that had traveled far
And my toughened toes with unbroken calluses,
Unspoken blemishes that weathered the storm.
Yet she washed the dirt from my calloused feet.

She neither smiled nor spoke to give away her thoughts
As she patiently washed the dirt from my tired feet.
I learned a long time ago that she was kind
And carried a large heart and a steady mind,
But did she always have that eternal patience
For each child who tugged at her dress,
Smile at the homeless who begged her for bread,
And like Peter gives all that she had.
A word of encouragement to warm the lonely heart.

I wished I could see deep into her soul
And rip a page to stuff my hollow hole.
Had she talked back to her mother when she had to
Or stolen a wear from her sister's shoes
To cover up her own calluses
And make her feet look beautiful?
Or had she lied about where she had been
To avoid a whipping for being bold growing up?
Or had she fundamentally been righteous from the start,
As in the picture she painted for me.

My heart upon her warm heart would lie
If I had looked her straight in the eyes
As she washed the dirt from between my toes
And without inhibition do a part on my own
As I didn't know how to ask to wash hers, too
And to let me dry her feet with my own locks
And anoint them with castor oil,
Break open her calluses, soothe the pain or let it be,
And continue the prayer in my heart
That I too may seek and speak for the voiceless,
Wash their feet, and give hope to those whose feet are bruised.

She Prayed for Us

Mothers are like passerines who sing and pray
And bring harmony and healing in the physical way.
Mothers perch and stay on their knees,
Planted there like the roots of ancient trees.
When there seems to be a rock blocking the way,
They pray for its removal as long as breath stays.

Mothers impel us to reach higher heights
Where our souls in comfort abide with delights,
Guide us as we traverse the mountain's peak,
Watch as we soar with open talons and beaks,
And then are gone before we have time to retreat
But leave us with the will to stand on our feet.

Mothers rocked our cradleboard by night and swept us into day.
They stayed by our sides until the dark clouds swept away
And with faltered emotion mixed with terror and fear
Created and molded our characters with sweat and tears.
Their breath grew roses where each teardrop fell
That bound our severed roots planted in Beckford Kraal.

She placed a poem in each of our hearts,
So we now write them in the rainbow
To ignite the sky for the world to glow.
From where blood-veined rivers flow,
We will remain on high, high above the cloud,
Until we write the lines in the sky and shout them out loud.

We mourned her passing but not without hope
And would rather call her back to nature to envision,
To give back a part of the heart she had given,
To sing back the songs she had sung to us,
To pray for her that last prayer she prayed for us,
And to shed that last tear she shed for us.

All the incendiary shocks crawled straight through us
As we sat in the pew and reminisced of her thoughtfulness
But if we can't, we will still sing and pray with our kids anyway,
Shout her praises loud from above the mountaintops
For the rest of the world to hear, know, and share,
For this was all she expected us to bear.

CHAPTER 2

THE JOYS OF MOTHERHOOD

The First Sunshine

How she glowed with delight
Every time her womb came alive.
Like a gleaming child with a lollipop,
She announced each time anew with pride.
And as 3,040 sunrises more popped,
She carried us with her every stride
Before setting us down to see
Just where the sunshine abides
And as each crucial moment slides,
When all our digits she could see,
Heaven's door opened, weight drifted,
And all anxiety and fear turned to glee.
And she smiled anew to see us wrenched
When the first ray bathed our innocent faces.

She Sang to Me

She sang to me in the silence of the womb,
In a cavern echoing deep when I couldn't see,
I could only feel the placating embrace,
Heard the soothing comfort of her voice,
Not knowing that was the sound of an overture
The ancient whispers travel here in cosmic waves.

She sang to me after I was begot
And brought me out into the cold air,
On a solid rock she planted my feet to stand
Not really the plan to step out on quicksand,
But paved the way for me to walk assured,
Less I kick my feet against the thorn of life.

She rocked my cradleboard through the night into day,
And stayed by me until the dark cloud swept away.
She molded my characters with her tears
To where I feel whole and free of fear
And the courage to stand up again after each fall
And fed my severed cord planted in Beckford Kraal.

She sang to me to invigorate my developing ego,
Songs her mother had sung to her ages ago.
Her songs held me high so on my own I could stand,
And for my first steps she held my hand,
Nourished my being, placed my feet on a rock
With patience to counteract the shock.

She placed a poem in my heart so I could write it on the rainbow
To ignite the sky for the world to glow,
From the mountaintop where blood-veined rivers flow
To the valley floor, flowing, carrying virtue far below.
But I remained on high, high above the cloud,
So I write her lines in the sky and shout them out loud.

She was gone before I had the chance to wish her farewell,
And I would rather call her back to envision her well,
To give back the part of the heart she had given me then
And sing back the songs she had sung to me.
But if I can't, I still will sing them anyway,
Shout out loud from above the mountain way
For the rest of the world to hear, know, and share!

An Incredible Being

Body and mind burst with pride and seraphic joy,
Miraculously transform before her very eyes,
Wrapped in a casing no change can destroy,
For next to the heart the innocence of life lies.
The stranger in the mirror smiles reassuringly.
Like a chrysalis morphs into a butterfly,
All virtues transform into motherhood,
Delicately poised in Isis's clothes for good.

Shame and pride disappear with shape,
Gone, lost in the privacy of giving birth,
Trapped in godliness that virtue cannot escape,
No longer uncomfortable in exposed skin.
Vagaries frozen with unclothed modesty,
The urge to nurture erodes shame so thin
And turns vulgarity into moral honesty.

When motherhood exhibits nature's best,
Nursing replaces decency in a feeding kit.
Catching a glimpse of an exposed breast,
Pride dissolves the mouth extracting that tit
And matches in godliness with a mother's wit,
For inside the kernel everything else fits.

The Virtuous Woman

How she lived, all she had done,
How she did it, no one knows. Only she alone.
Heaven blessed her plenty with fecundity,
And for endurance she looked above.
She molded and nurtured us into perfect bloom,
Nourished us straight from her very womb.

For ninety-nine months and more,
Where each incremental nine months
Stayed to recap the one gone before
And reproduced the trauma she bore
Only to repeat the cycle again,
She protected and sheltered us from the rain.

Throughout the times when we seemed to not want to make it,
The sleepless nights she watched us over
And prayed with all the faith she had to spare,
Trickled tears mixed with agony and fear
That death would steal us away in the night.
As the darkness faded and dawn broke light
She fell asleep with the tempest in her arms,
For in her mind the light protects from harm.

For swiping the snot from our running noses
And catching the cold that relieved our woes,
She did it all and gave her all
But never put down a payment recall,
And where the crops fell,
She caught the bits with delight
And sang painful praises as well
For the obscurity concealed in the night.

The Matriarch

Bigger than life she stood shrouded with blood,
A pillar of strength towered over to do us good,
A matriarch that bridged the scattered pieces
And reassembled her children from far places.

She annexed them to live in order to be exemplified,
Built the heirloom by which we all are identified
With compelling adhesion that glued us together.
Until her will is done, we stoop for nothing else.

Stronger than life, the calcium in our backbones,
Unwavering love encased in bones as rigid as stone,
Is the determination that embedded in us the will to survive,
Unfazed by obstacles, undaunted in perpetual drive.

Toughness, inherently stringent, flooded her bloodline
And against all odds pressed to maintain the family line
Regardless of the momentous hills she had to climb—
A willpower that never faltered through intrepid time.

Through the archives of time maintained an aura of invincibility,
Love in a strength that personified courageous invulnerability,
Not time, open space, or death can uproot the tree she planted
Nor generation gap annihilates the memorabilia she mounted.

A matriarch that bridges the scattered pieces,
Heaves the splinters to mend the broken slices,
Our mother lives unbending, straight as an arrow,
The backbone of all who descend over time.

Home Again

She learned everything about parenting from the books she read,
From those she bought because she thought she had not been sufficiently fed
By those her mother bought because she thought she hadn't given enough
To plug a hollow depth, a desire only to fill it up.
She read age-appropriate books to her in the womb,
Not knowing what she knew and could not assume.
Hoping she would grow up feeling adequately good,
And so she read and read everything she could.

What the books did not tell her,
Was what wasn't written or conferred,
Was that she too had changed. Like her growing up,
The little one would grow up and prosper unscathed
And behave just as she too had behaved,
Make her own choices in things she acquires herself,
Learn to creep by no one else,
Balance on her feet before she takes the first step.

But what the books had also not told her
Was that there would be shrinking and expansion too,
That she and everything else would shrink,
And with all the worries it would be hard not to think
That expansion would erase the memories
Of the many gallons of milk they produced
For once the milk and needs were gone,
Once the food factory became history
Then she began to remember the story
But couldn't remember where she heard it first,
What it's like to sleep again alone with guilt dispersed.

When she looks in the mirror and recognizes the frame that's hers
And a stranger stares at her,
She begins to feel a feeling of belonging and desire,
For the body that was hers before the change,
Her attitude had already changed once the innocence was gone.
Everything changes, grows, not staying the same,
Weights awkwardly shift in places she don't want to claim
Like the changing mother she never met
Whose loneliness she wears still without regret.

First the hollow space and the desire,
Her mouth again became tasty and watery
For the things she didn't remember having a taste for,
Like sipping a glass of white wine at nine
In the sereneness of the night when all are asleep
And the desire to go dancing again to change this
And a craving for a taste of the things that were tasteless.
To ignore the smell of alcohol on his breath
And think it's all right even if it doesn't taste minty.

When she can list the things she never thought she'd do,
Like let her child cries herself to sleep
Or fall when she betrays her watch and keep
And chose to look away because she needs to look away
Or let her spend the weekend at her mother's
And not bear the thought of abandonment
Or mention breasts many times in the casual way,
She thinks they were never hers in the first place
And all trivial things of being are gone from her face.

When the space around becomes obvious in visible amounts,
Spaces she never thought was there to count,
Now she counts them as if she was seeing them for the first time,
Wondering how they got to be prime:
Forty-nine rolled-up dirty diapers tossed in a trash can,
Twenty-three dirty dishes piled in the sink,
Four piles of laundry—one more than the number people living in the house.
How are there so many covers for so few bodies?
Two strollers, two car seats, and two others,
How does everything double when there is only one you?
Three cribs, one at her mother's house,
How did they ever get here?

The purpose of which she is still unsure,
Where has she been and for how long?
She now drives in the car without the smell of leather
And still counts spaces while shrinking underneath.
Then she drives up to her house,
Strange, as if she is seeing it for the first time.
It looks like a neighbor passing by,
And she thinks to herself, it sure seems warm inside.

CHAPTER 3

CARES OF MOTHERHOOD

The Worry of a Mother

She worried not for herself but for us all,
How to give lives to the ones she brought.
Days she pondered how we'd ever survive,
Every wake she prayed for one more to live.
Each night she paraded singing songs of praise
For the blessing of another day.
Incrementally satisfied at heart,
She refused to see beyond today.
In the back of her mind, she fought
The fear, the hideous task ahead,
The dreary days, the bleak nights,
Filled with the same gruesome dread.
But somehow in the crevice of time it connects,
And the dark coalescence clouds merge to protect.

Our Mother, Indeed!

Mothers always write in shorthand pencil.
Everything else can be erased or stenciled.
Plans and schedules do have their place.
The laundry list can wait, the grooming postpone.
Some will have to be shelved in cloud space,
For nothing is greater than becoming a mother.
Fearlessly conforming to the role they've been given
When nature takes precedence over all things,
And this, my friend, is not hormone driven

The marathon of care stretches as time lasts
Watches until the last love-bundle is fast asleep.
Motherhood is engrained with strength and courage
Like a cougar that stands alert in a guardian keep,
For the safety of her cubs is presciently complete.
Nothing stands between her and their needs
That she wouldn't drain from herself to meet.
And these, my friend, are our mothers indeed!

Mothering Care

She shelters us from the stormy ring,
And like a kangaroo she wears a sling
To erase the choice between chores
And nurture in the same time core,
To keep our food warm and hygienic,
An instinct to protect more than eugenics
As she adjusts to our shape and shade
In her elements, unabashed, unafraid.

Yet the only reward she expects in return
Is the satisfaction to see a healthy growth.
She watches us thrive as the clock turns;
Our every move and intention counts.
She bubbles with glee and happiness
As our development buds with success,
Joy that plainly makes her heart crest
And literally bulge out her chest.

She thinks ahead, steels our every need,
Adjusts to changes at lightning speed.
Omnipresent, 24-7,
An incredible gift given from heaven.
She instinctively gives care as a mammalian does
And is always there no matter what the time says,
That heaven deep-rooted in her DNA.
And this, my friend, is our destiny's way.

The Other Side of Coping

When Jeff died, the inner side of her closed.
She locked him in her deepest closet
And would not let him out again.
Though she locked up all grief and pain,
I could hear him stomping on the floor
Because I was always at the door.

And since I was that close,
I could see the silent tears flow.
Obliviously, she spoke to him daily
When she thought she was all alone.
Sometimes it started with a groan.
I know because I was always there.

Sometimes out of the clear blue sky
Came the groan and then the mumbling
Just like when she spoke to her God
In a tongue that He alone understood.
Then she turned to me and said, "That's Jeff;
He tossed a stone my way to let me know he's here."

Her voice was a silvery disembodied undertone,
The one she used when she spoke in tongues
Or when she communicated with ghosts,
Those rice watered eyes alone could see.
Now I guess she was speaking to them
Because there was no one else there.

She always wanted me close,
As if afraid that I too would go
And the dead would rise and intercede
As demented fate swooped down to feed,
For she blamed it on herself still,
For letting the ghost of Uncle Richard in.

The Mothers Who Raised Me

I am the son of the mothers, but these I claim.
The mothers of all times, the triune of reality,
Separate characters and values fused in one aim,
Love, purity, and respect all the same,
Because they first loved me anew.
Everything they do is to propel me through.

The mother who fathered me here,
Gave birth to me, and placed me on solid ground,
Whose everything I bear and carry around the place,
Complete with the facial expression I share—
She gave me love that follows me through
Along with the values she instilled in me.
As I matured, I realized how much of her I carry.
This I'll pass to my children so they too may pass it.

The mother who advanced my career,
The one I ran to when my needs were not met,
Who gave me money when to school I had to go,
Smiled and encouraged me in everything I did—
When my school days seemed over,
She found me a job to keep me inspired,
One that brought me independence and confidence.

The mother who adopted my emotion,
Geared me along the path that led to here,
Bolstered my morale and my self-esteem too—
She stayed with me until I could stand composed,
And then she too was gone, transition into time
Before I had time to retreat and recompense.
But she left me with the will to seek and speak
So I can write unabashed. For this too I am grateful.

Mothers of the Earth

Mothers of the earth,
The place of our birth,
How can we just stand there
And not share the pain they bear?

If you look, you'll see it in their eyes.
If you listen, you'll hear it in their cries.
If you care, you will not just stand there
But share their pains with the world.

They build our characters on solid rocks
And place them in our hearts in concrete blocks.
But there can be no glory, no honor in strength,
If we can't uphold theirs beyond a generation's length

And present them to the world
As queens in jewelry impearled.

CHAPTER 4

CHANGES/FAITH

It Never Stops Raining

Meticulously prearranged and precisely put together,
The cycle of births and deaths brings renewed capabilities,
So that one day should cyclically follow another
In a routine loop of life. Just what is another possibility.

Wednesday followed by Thursday, Friday, and Saturday
That one should wake up in the bleak morning's smother.
Like a broken record, time resets in second chances each day
And then ends a cycle of life to where it first began into another.

Contently in came Jeff, like the emergence of a tulip in spring.
Rough but enough, life endures all, the joy that births bring.
But then by twelve he exited the front door,
And it became devastatingly cold.

Her life was a bubbly routine mixed with complex certainty,
But that was her routine. She lived it daily shadowed in doubt.
When she thought it was getting better, satisfied with its casualty—
Boom!—it took another turn and unexpectedly took her out.

Just when she thought the rain would stop pouring
And she could see the blue sky from where she stood, groping,
Rannie swung down from the Mataga tree and was the fourth to go,
And the dark cloud reappeared and blocked her view.

Expectation stayed stable in a handful of sifting sand.
If one stayed around, one learned from her how to let go,
How to hold on tight but not with a clenched fist.
Jonathan was the first and left her for a foreign land.
Vin followed suit on the wings of the morning mist.

Gladston tried to go but had no leg on which to stand,
So he stuck around long enough until her untimely death.
Boysie stayed and she thought that was all she had to bond.
Each day was a nagging reminder that he too would go.

After that, all visual emotions were swept under the shadows,
How unpredictable little deaths were thought recognizable;
How she loved or resented, experienced joy and pain—no one knows.
Yet her emotions doused with feelings were undecipherable.

Even though she might have died many times before,
These deaths and rebirths must come to an absolute end.
How did she ever endure them all? No one knows for sure
How she cherished the many instances when love descended.

Birth and death, joy and mirth, all in the evolution of time,
But does it matter, as living must inevitably cease completely
And everything else will cyclically go on with or without her?
Or is it consoling to believe that this death ends it all, absolutely?

Strength and Resilience

Her strength and ingenuity came from the one above,
Descended, unseen, masked in the shadow of a dove,
Each day a reminder of the one precariously proceeded
That gave rise to new challenges of societal precedent.

Hungry mouths to feed but no sight of any fish or bread,
A monthly lease to pay to keep the roof hung over our head,
The anxiety for good advice to develop a solid foundation,
Food, books, schools, clothes, the very cost of education.

All lingered as she brooded, but she still maintained the courage.
In uncertainty, the unknown clung on like hope in bondage.
The capacity to give the mite shoved her to share the loaf
And give up bits of herself when the portion ran aloof.

With repeated resilience she trekked over the many years
But persistently sustained everything she could ever bear.
For us she repeated it over again, selflessly and without regard.
From us she expected nothing but sincerity as her reward.

Love is strength and resilience in the making of a mother.
No one else continuously repeats the cycle without a bother.
In those bones is encased a love that spreads beyond family borders.
Today her spirit lives in all those who proudly call her mother.

CHAPTER 5

COMING TO GRIPS WITH SELF

Disengagement

In the darkened womb where I began
Poured into me the substance of man.
Buoyant in amnion fluid so I floated
Embraced with confidence so I bloated.

I could not see or breathe, but I could move.
With each move she felt nothing else to prove
But fed into me the gambit of life,
Preparing me to stand on my own.

Through the agony of human birth
I was forced out to encounter earth,
To take the first breath on my own,
And make my first steps all alone

She watched as I would stumble and fall,
Lent a hand to raise an honor call,
Morally defined and physically grown
Until I gathered the wit to stand on my own.

How I Remembered My Father

I could not remember when he left.
I was there but too young to know when.
Gone: this I remember not like the rest.
Absence: the only thing that was evident of him then.

My mother was tough; she carried it around in a rigid face
Concealed in the burden she bore and carried around the place.
It must have been rough to be mother and father all the time,
But if it was ever unbearable, she never did show.

No grave, no poverty dampened the strength deep inside.
I still recall the only time I saw her break down and cry;
It was when my brother tied the cow in the field of crops
We had planted just to put food on the tabletop.

The hurt I felt inside made me cried too
Just to see what she had to go through,
But I never forgave my brother
For putting her through such pain,
More than she could bear in vain.

She never spoke of him in the present tense.
I cannot remember her ever speaking of him at all
Except the time I took the airmail home from the post office.
She dropped the knife and the breadfruit she was peeling,
Wiped her hands on her apron, and took the letter.

She held it for a long while, staring down at it
With a stoic expression. She appeared to be reading it unopened.
She was in no rush to open it as she always had been before
And treated it like a telegram, fearful of what it might say.
I didn't know what to make of her then

Because I had never seen that expression before,
But then she turned to me and said, "Johnathan is coming home."

But he didn't abandon us, or did he?
He didn't die? I could still hear his voice
And see his indescribable face in my dreams.
He just hopped out on us
In search of a better life
Where he thought the grass was greener.

It was after World War II killed most of the able men
And England wanted laborers to rebuild its economy.
Being from the Commonwealth, he didn't need a visa
And he was one of the early Windrush generation.
He sailed to England on one of those banana boats,
The very way he returned because he was afraid to fly.

I remember the time I caught the cold.
My chest heaved and fried like egg in hot oil.
Some chicken soup he scooped
And tried to feed me with a spoon.
"Haaa, haaa," he said, his mouth wide open.
"Take a sip, my little tumble bug."
I opened my mouth to let in a spoonful.
Soon I finished the whole cup of soup,
Just a spoonful at a time.

I still can't remember what he looked like then,
But this I knew: I heard his voice all too well,
Every time my memory jolted me back there.
Like when he wiped the cold from my running nose,
Sang me a lullaby, and with some smelling herbs,
He placed under my nose, cleared my lungs to a quiet repose
The thought of his mystical healing makes me smile even now.

I still recall his hand, a rough measure of tenderness,
And the way he held the spoon and guided it to my mouth.
The flame of discipline he trusted through my growth
Still burns my heart and nourishes me to the end.
Although he opted in vanished ages, when I grew
His spirit controlled me, comforted me,
Guiding me, nourishing me.

The Tears

Terror ejects fear. Too dumb to speak.
Tears flowed downward in silent stream.
No sob, no hiss, no murmur, no peek.
Current emotions folded back to redeem.
They trickled and meandered down the cheek
To the edge of the chin and over the cliff,
Drained the tar from a cluttered mind.
Sister Nin, with a white handkerchief,
Derailed the path, mopped the tears dry
And wiped away the grime from the trail,
And the riverhead became as barren as a nail.
No geyser, no stream for good, no waterfall,
Only a pleasant memory that stood out tall.
Now I know that she did not go anywhere.
She is here and with a white handkerchief
Wiped dry the tears from my eyes
With a whisper that assured, "It's all right. I am here."

A Package of Handkerchiefs

I closed my eyes to not see her face,
But as I folded back the hoods to see,
Two streams shot out with a hiss in a race
And flowed downstream like creeks,
Columns of water tumbling down to meet
And turn into a fall at the end of each cheek.

Sister Nin with a white handkerchief
Saw the hurt, the pain, and the grief
Well up like hot springs bursting for release.
Years of anguish now rested in peace.
Tears drained the source at the head
And then stopped the flow as it sped.

My mind raced back to when
I traveled home from college then
Expecting money but none she had.
Disappointed, I left for the square
To wait for a bus to take me back there,
Thinking what a fool I had been
To have used up my last to get me there.

Bob came running down the street
And handed me a package so neat.
"It's from Mama," he said as a greet.
There it was, a package of handkerchiefs
Neatly folded as they came in the pack
In colors of bright yellow, green, and black.

The message I never did understand,
But it all rushed back to me in the stand,
Where I stood in grief, sorry for all of us there.
"Wipe the tears from your eyes," she whispered.
"It's all right. I am here."

Intrinsic Will of Being

A note generates, especially in the holiday season.
I send one to each of my siblings for the same reason.
That despite our daily struggles, having our core values tested
Reminds us that we are vulnerable, not invincibly poured,
And life's strain we can endure if ourselves we share.

As time passes, our corpus faculties erode,
But intact is our intrinsic will of being,
Precariously displayed but strategically posed
To spread that which inheritance imposed
From Papa, Mama, and the ancestral pool,
Giving meaning to how our genes unfolded.

You pass through as the conduit but still too the link
That connects the family line with yesterday and now.
But you too must graciously and instinctively step aside
For Floyd, Abe, Oral, and June to be included
And instill in them the value of our lineage,
For to their descendants they too must pass it.

But first you must complete your task inherited
And assure your siblings that the protégée too has to act.
To Gladston, Vin, and Dee, their part still remains intact.
To Ronnie, Jean, and Dotty, they stride at the same pace.
To Joyce, Boysie, and Sonie, they too tread in line
To perform their parts and seal Mama's abiding pact.

We don't have eternity or immortality apart
And must give closure, as we too must part.
Then and only then can you amiably go,
As you must first erase your crease, set ages ago,
Where crevices undyingly underlined Mama's face.

The Old Tombstone

We loaded into two vehicles
To look for old Mama Mary
And repeat the same old miracle.
All steadfast, none got weary,
Our attention glued on the vase
Riveted into the old tombstone,
In its chamber long dead flowers out of place.
Tombed there in the cold and all alone, lay
Mary Theodosia Wilson, 1922–2010,
And her daughter retold the same old tale.
Surely it would happen again, she said.
The last encounter was no fluke, just fate.
She asked her to acknowledge again
If she had heard her well
And put the sign in the plastics flower once more,
Where empty infinite spaces dwelled.
Wilted doubts sat still in the vase,
Listened for breaks in the still air,

Swirling images of an invisible face.
We stood our ground
All eyes fixed on the vase
As the flowers swirled around
And made a new revolution.
So it was for all to see.
It's no fluke; it's a revelation.
But the Wilsons were not amused,
For they knew too well
That old Mama Mary could hear as well.

Thursday Night

The wind stood still and absorbed her last breath.
Taunting feelings, flaunting thoughts I dreaded,
Slowly slipping away between my fingers
Like a handful of sifting sand lingers.
I said a silent prayer for her,
For the wind not to take away her breath.
I felt the answer, and my heart dropped.
A nauseous feeling inside me openly flopped.
I heard the voice, but the words were unspoken.
I knew then that she was gone,
And I too in earnest tried to hurry on.

I desperately tried to give in, to get to her,
But she would not let me out in the storm.
The pain, the anguish became unbearable,
Piercing my wounded side repeatedly.
As my dreams struggled to stay relevant,
I felt like wind trapped in the sail,
Unable to further propel the ship.
Meanwhile, inside me the storm still raged
As I laid there, disturbed, on one side,
Unable to move to the other.
But I just had to get to her somehow.

Like a burning candle left out on the tray,
In liquid wax, a light burned-out wick,
I spent Thursday night unveiling and unraveling
A restless storm, calming the burning wounds,
Crawling in and out of my psyche
Like a continuum of lopsided pendulums
Hanging on the brink of my thoughts,
Trembled at the fear of being baked again,
A fire, toasting my dreams all over my brain.

The unyielding wound that kept me in bed bleeding,
Suffocating, sweating against the sheets, dreaming,
Searching for the balance to my dyslexic pattern.
Strewn across the canvas of my brain,
Compensated by the cause, I found the remains
I had to reach across. I had to get to her.

Barbed wire tore into my thoughts,
Ripping my flesh, refusing to let me free.
I kept seeing her tired face smiling at me,
Lying on her side, refusing to go to sleep.
I won't soon forget the tempest in those eyes.
And then it was Friday.
You walked through the opening of my cell
And told me the recipient had died.

CHAPTER 6

ASSURANCE

We Will Be All Right

Mom, although you have moved on
To a higher place where saints congregate,
A plane that transcends human perspective,
Where temporal dimensions cede to spiritual forms,
Where tears and sorrows surrender to blissfulness
And pain, suffering, and worries exist no more,
You can still watch our every move
As our destinies unfold and we do what we must
And aspire to live upright and do what is just.
Like you, Mom, our deeds will ascend us in place.
So you can now close your eyes and sleep in peace,
Rest assuredly and smile with boastful contentment,
Not because you are now with the earlier saints
But because you know that we too will be all right.

A Pitcher of Red Wine

Unusual to go to the well after noon when the sun is still high,
But that's what I did to fetch a pitcher of water.
By the wall of the well in the shadows,
A stranger, a figure silhouetted against the light,
Appeared like a god out of the sunlit sky
And stood staring out the distance, gazing at nothing,
Expectantly staring at me, undressing me, shedding my shawl,
Penetrating my world and luring me out of the confines of my walls.

A rudimentary voice echoed in the realm of my mind,
His voice, a whisper, a murmur in the calm of the wind.
So I went over and said, "Pardon me." My voice cracked open.
His eyes, my eyes, four eyes met only for a moment,
Sharp, laser-like, dissecting. I began to melt like butter on a hot platter,
Moist, wet, perspiration, nakedness, out of the shower, dripping water,
His face, that face, peaceful, serene, almost angelically fixed,
His eyes beckoning me. I remained transfixed,
Locked in that hypnotizing stare, completely spellbound,
Descending in gravitational free fall, astoundingly confounded
To where I was driven into total submission,
Feeding into my slavish desire and inhibition.

For a brief moment I thought he was crying,
For I saw bloodlike tears roll down his cheeks,
Fear, tears, and sweat blended but agonizingly undying.
What my mind beheld, words couldn't speak.
His lips cracked opened. He asked me for a drink of water.
I hesitated, for he was a stranger and I a Samaritan
And such was the custom in these quarters,
But I was hypnotized, mesmerized, and dumbfounded.
I gave him the pitcher of water anyway,
And as his lips parted to drink, drops of blood

Rolled down his cheeks and mixed with the water.
He gave the pitcher back to me and said, "Drink."
I looked in at the red wine and then up at his face.
He said, "If you drink you will never thirst again."
So I drank and drank and drank until I floated high,
So high my mind floated around my brain.
I closed my eyes to keep him and the feeling inside,
In this warm embrace that was ripping me apart.

Then he broke the trance and asked me for my man friend,
And I lied because I thought it was the right thing to do,
But he told me of the first that I had screwed
And the others that had screwed me
And threaded my life in the open space,
Ripped the lid off my dark corner, where I hid the ugly ones.
I became afraid, panicking at his detailed, in-depth knowledge.
I dropped the pitcher and fled into town to alert my neighbors:
"Come see a man who lives across time and space."
But when we returned, he was nowhere to be found.
Only the pitcher of red wine sat on the wall,
The wall of the well that Jacob built with his hands
And the inscription written in chalk coal:
"The Messiah born of a woman out of the loins of Abraham."

A Cosmic Assurance

You left us here among the chaos,
But I learned that you never truly leave.
You crossed into that velvet galaxy
Where I still hear you loud and clear.

And when I am in a pensive mood,
I look up among the stardust
And see you all twinkling there,
Smiling at me, telling me it's all right.

When I think about your inevitable grave
And that final song of breath you gave,
I am assured that since you went,
There will be a place for me to rent
Because your faith in the eternal one
Will find us security when there is none.

When I close my eyes,
I dream of where you are
And want to be there too,
If only for a day or two,
To circle the cosmos as star dust
In that impossible ethereal zone.

Basal Shoots

Siblings are like suckers attached to
The same womb, where all were dispatched.
Like coupling lizards they remained latched
Long after the fruits matured and dispersed,
And the old trunk gave up of herself first
After her youthfulness was spent giving nurse,
Lingers in a state of not dying but living ends
That all can latch together as life support lends.

Cling on with kisses, care, and salted cheeks,
With dried tear tracks under cosmetic tweaks
And slit lips with a bitter tongue
And rotten words sometimes flung.
Spit out in accepted comical satire,
Bloody cloth dresses words in neat attire,
Waiting at the end of the line on needles and pins
To the boundary where love ends and terror begins.

At the border is the red line,
Penetrated but clearly defined
Like the placental membrane
Attaches, its nurtured, its nourished but separates.
All the attached tolerances that love generates
Delicately balance with contempt all the same
From a consuming fire petered into a gentle flame.

But when the fire consumes the red line
And you step outside your confines,
Exposing harsh contempt without respect,
There are consequences and side effects.
Complacency will no longer stay the course
When the intrinsic bonds that kept us gullibly intact
Are ruptured, severed and broken apart, irreparable.

When you have gone that far
And the irreconcilables are dissolved
And the cops get involved
To read you your rights,
Take their advice and be nice.
It's your right to dispatch.
Wean and let go. You are on your own.
Dispatch, you just got to let go
So we can again attach, separately.

Look Up for Me

Don't search for me among the corpses
Nor where they place the dead.
You will never find me there,
For I am everywhere else
Among the living.

Don't look for me among the grains of sand
Or among the mounds of grave land
Where the headstone reminds you of death.
Just look for me among the heavens,
For I am in spirit world, home in unwearied rest.

Don't search for me among earthlings.
Like the resurrection, I too moved on,
To pave another path for the disenchanted.
As I go, I leave you the will to seek and speak
And the spirit to remind you of the path to follow.

So search for me out there in the starscape,
For I am one of many in the Milky Way.
I crossed over into that spiral galaxy,
So look up among the stardust.
You'll see me twinkling there.

Inevitably So

Everything slows to a halt, slipping.
Time slows when relativity clicks in,
The earth stops revolving,
And the years stop counting,
Yet she stays the same and feels the same:
Hope, dreams, and the desire stay, even her fame.
Her nights linger, tinkering on stars
and planets and space and home.
She wants the world to know before she goes,
Wants to slow the progression, but finds she can't.
She was light-years ahead, but time ran out.
I try to keep up with her, to hold on to her
like smoke in my hands.
I thought I could, I promised I would,
But she slips through my fingers like sifting sand
And transitions into outer space for good.
I keep looking up to see her beyond the clouds
And hope that she will return.
She crossed the spiral galaxy where mortals are not allowed,
And like all relics, I have to wait my turn.

CHAPTER 7

NOW AND HEREAFTER

Just Yesteryear

Just yesteryear this old rugged frame
Was cartilaginous and pliable.
Just yesteryear this old rugged frame
Was full of hope and promise,
Admirable in its youthful perfection,
Like tulip blossoms popping up in early spring.

Today the affliction of time
Has weathered it into a rigid,
Brisk, calcium-starved frame.
Today these mortal bones,
Ridged, two hundred and six,
Crumbling, fused, and fixed
Have lost their contractibility,
Encased in a loosed inelastic sheet.

Just yesterday this old rugged frame
Housed the most glamorous incandescent figure
That personified the qualities and virtues
Of the feline feminine persona.
Today all this had worn out
From the trivial steps of life.

Just yesterday this old rugged frame
Created and transformed
So many lives, including mine.
Once so appealingly attractive,
Endearingly charming in an angelic stature,
Today a sculpture of a lifeless corpse.

This old rugged frame,
The creation of the perfection of God,
An instrument that bore,
Produced, and recreated
The fruit of God's wish and desire.

Don't Cry For Me When I Am Gone

Come on now. Wipe your weeping eyes.
I am here, ready to go, so don't cry alone.
As surely as the sun goes down in the western sky,
God did not place me here to turn to stone.

I hear the whisper of the wind, "Come home!"
It's my Savior calling me over. "Come on home!"
His signal is the wind. "Come. Your tenure here is done."
I must go alone, so don't cry for me when I am gone.

Release me. Tell me it is all right. Let me cross over.
Listen! You can hear it too. Whistle the wind's atone.
Look! It's my Savior's outstretched hand. "Come over!"
So don't you all dare cry for me when I am gone.

I must go now. I must answer to the call.
While I am gone, don't cry for me at all.

Going Home

Wipe the tears from your eyes. The time has come
For me to leave this body behind and go home.
Look at me! What you see here will not last.
And the way you feel now, it too will pass.
Nothing is permanent, and my life was not set in stone.
My work here is done. Now I travel alone.
He called me today: "Come to the home
That I diligently prepared for you. Come!
Your tenure in mortality is done."
Though I leave my body, I am not really gone.

Like tattered rags, the shell I left in decline
Is like the exoskeleton the snake left behind.
This old frame served me well while it lasted,
But it is weathered with the affliction of its past.
Until the resurrection and life, it too I must part.
So cherish the memories I left within your heart,
For God the merciful protector secures my soul.
This He will reunite with the body in perfect whole.
So grieve for a while, if grieve you must,
But let your heart be comforted by trust.

The Journey Home

For all she gave, heaven was her final abode.
The journey to collect a just reward took her there
After her heart was weighed against the feather of truth.
Migrated in time to where she cherished so dear,
Where mass and burden are denuded to naught,
Into a weightless expansion of timeless space,
She journeys alone beyond the star she sought.

She traveled where no distance is far, high, or wide,
Where depth is neither deep or unfathomably placed,
Where light-years and nautical expanses absorb into space,
Where no grave, no tomb, no concrete can hold her down.
Like termites, she burrowed up, borrowed wings, ready to soar.
From underground, subterranean, where termites refuse to bore,
Into open space she soared to collect floating dreams.
She journeys alone to her final abode.

A journey to the castle at the end of the universe,
In space beyond earth's stars and floating moons,
Where thoughts immerse and dreams traverse
And time suspends and the moments come this soon,
Where souls are animated and worries vanished away,
Beyond this place into space where lives rupture no more,
A place where hope joins faith to send love ones on before
A journey into heavenly stream, where souls rest evermore.

An Old Rugged Frame

In the shining casket rests this old rugged frame,
Weathered, tired bones showing wear and tear,
Adorable but endearing, withstanding all blame.
A dusty frame, brittle, freckled, and bare
That endured a life not without trials but in trust travailed
And survived this world with suffering but also with dignity prevailed.

This old rugged frame once so admired, so respected,
Wore the cloth of dignity like a shining armor,
Bore the persona of a wondrous affinity projected.
Now lifeless, comatose, it rests in the parlor,
But in the dark cellar this old frame must first abide,
For only a spell in the cell, goals the ascension goad.

This old rugged frame, wrapped in burial shroud
That proudly covers all blemishes and physical imperfections.
Dispersed, the storm rests like a solitary cloud
Once full of wisdom and flawless perfection,
Resting in this solitary divine mortal frame
Until that day when her soul revives this claim.

Stained and scarred, this old rugged frame stood so saintly,
Bore the insignia of beauty and purity tethered together.
This old rugged frame left this legacy, shunned so daintily
A trove of trophies bequest in perpetual love forever
To be the beacon of the path we must bear and share,
For in our hearts she'll always be that alarming flare.

Today we'll not mourn over this old rugged frame.
We'll wait until the fulfillment of her story.
We'll cling to her memoirs, legend, and fame
Until that day when we all meet up in glory.
We'll guard the trophies she long laid down
And patent them to the realm of her crown.

It Hurts to Say Goodbye

In our hearts we grieve to part with your council.
All you ever asked was to be God-fearing,
To live upright, to be just to others,
To not be bashful, to be humble, and to give thanks always,
Knowing blessings transcend unseasonably.

The warm, unconditional, universal love
That you poured over us and everyone else
Caught on like virus with those you impacted,
Not only those who bear your genes
But also all who came into contact with you.

We'll follow your footsteps wherever they lead.
We'll cherish the memories you left us.
Your soft sweet voice in words of wisdom
Remain ringing in our ears like the chapel bell
And provide us with the comfort we need so well.

You prepared our hearts as we watched you go,
And through your own words we understood why.
"God did not place us here on earth to turn stones"
Was an assurance that your tenure on earth was done.
Thank you, Mama, for being our mother.

CHAPTER 8

SUCCESSION

The Transfiguration

Mama defied the logic of mortal death.
Her spirit ascended, enlightenment attained.
For her, death could not contain.
I looked for her in the casket-ware.
She wasn't there, but in us she was everywhere.
As I look at you, I see her, double jeopardy all over.

I did not see her go. Did you see it done?
I left her there. How could she have gone?
I didn't hear her say goodbye to me, to you, to us.
Now I can feel her there, here; she is everywhere.
We did not bury her. She was not there.
Why didn't I look at you, my dear?

Mama's spirit lives in you, in me, in us.
She lives in us ten times over all at once.
But most of all she transfigures, living through you.
Now, you embody her personality, you embrace her suffering,
You give her shape, form, and texture, you relive her humility,
And you provide her the peace that transcends her to eternity.

Now her spirit transcends the power of immortality,
And we owe it to ourselves to ensure her will be done.
God knows in you He finds favor to carry it on
And makes you the custodian that embodies her glories.
Sister Nin, live, but if you should go before we all are fed,
Pass her on. She's mine, she's yours, our embodiments.

Her Will Be Done

Is it the transmigration of her spirit to yours?
The transfiguration of her soul to your soul?
The resurrection of her body renewed in yours?
Reincarnation metamorphosed here in sight,
Logics defy reasoning, and all sense of realism submerge.
Call it Timbuktu. All I see is a mystic clone resurging.

From this chaotic rumble, jumble, frenzy of deportment,
Emerges a symbol that embodies her benevolence.
The ills of life or the sting of death could not erase her intent
To perpetuate living so that we might live more affluently.
She choose you to complete what she no longer could contain
And charged you to carry that mantle until we all are fed.

Mama lived yesterday in the shadows of herself,
And what you saw was just what you got alone,
For beyond that veil was a determined heart of stone
That would not give in even to life's most tragic adversaries.
When she could no longer hold on, she elected you
So her spirit could live on as a guiding light to us all.

The finality of death could not consume her life.
What she lived for would not have been immortalized
But would have suffocated in the absence of a surrogate
And remain inaccessible at the midpoint to eternity
If it couldn't be transferred through humanity.
Thank God in you a conveyance was found.

CHAPTER 9

BEAUTY AND PURITY

Contents of Characters

Mama, the legacy you left behind will never die.
It will be immortalized through generations to come,
Forever beholden to a bond that binds and ties
Because every bit of what we today have become
Is ensconced in how you raised us.

We'll relive your life and cherish our upbringing,
Hold on to the contents in the characters you gave us.
Your faith in God taught us to believe in ourselves,
Your strong courage translated into the strength we have,
And your industrious ways channeled our independence.

Your humility and great sense of humor attracted others to you.
Your kind and caring attitude stimulated our sensitivity to others.
The way you expressed gratitude challenged us to be humble.
But most of all, it was the sharing of your love with all
That gave us the blessing today to be who we are.

You never judged but always encouraged and accepted us
For who we were, and you were proud of what we became.
The pride you showed when we achieved,
The sparkle in your eye as you expressed thanks
Gave us the confidence to achieve even more.

And as you take that final journey home,
We just want you to know that the seeds you've sown
Have not all fallen on barren soil like others
But have blossomed to replicate the seeds you bore.
Pleasant journey, Mom. We'll meet you in glory yonder.

Beautiful Mama

Beauty is only skin deep, they say.
Peel it away and her beauty still stays
Intact, a personality that soothes like a river stone
Smoothed by the current in perfect tone.

Beauty is not what is seen but what is perceived.
Just peel away the layer and feed into its creativity.
Hidden behind the clutter in the crock of culture,
An ideal beauty lies even in a peel-headed vulture.

Beauty is only in the eyes of the beholder, they say.
But her beauty is not the suit she is wearing today.
Appearance only complements what lies beneath,
Exposes the confidence in the good of everyone, just to unsheathe.

Beauty transmutes into kindness and elegance,
Transcends the body, cosmetic and all physical features
Into a state of mind, as abstract as spirituality and as concrete as love
But only the beauty of a mother transcends all case in time.

Nothing to Compare

Nothing as selfless, as sacred,
As consecrated, as revered.

Nothing on earth to compare to her love,
Not even the love descended in a dove.

No love as genuine as resilience,
Not for a moment her love wanes.

She'll do anything and everything for all
And laid down her life at our beck and call.

She molds our characters and shapes our futures too,
Gives meaning to nothingness and fills the void.

She is a valued gift, God's best donation,
His dearest pottery in His prized creation.

She is the wave that danced away the day
Into tomorrow to continue into the bay.

She is a pleasure, an experience that never ends.
No one and nothing else can dare compare to then.

Getting off the Brink

A bold glimmer of light, alight.
The evening filled with flickering stars.
Darkness fills the night with delight.
Sparkles, light the darkness from afar.

I woke from my slumber unprepared,
The nightmare gone, leaving me intone.
I can breathe, fresh air I can share,
The crap fell from my throat on its own.

I am off the ledge, but I float in space,
For I am still standing on the brink.
My mind must catch up and interface,
Waiting for it to fall in so I can think.

I climb down the mountain stairwell.
There's a frightful delay, and I have the dilemma—chill.
Weary of every step and out of my shell,
On solid ground fear draws nearer still.

I am still petrified on solid ground,
Too long impounded on the brink alone.
I have to learn how to live unwound.
I have to teach me how to get stone.

I could do with some assurance.
Just one thing left for me to try.
I am running out of clearance.
I have to teach me how to fly.

Today Is All I Have

Today is all there is.
I must catch the last glimpse of the crepuscular rays
Before they escape into the creeping purple shadows
As they pace their way to the other side of today.
So I watch the sunset from my back porch
As it sneaks away beyond the leaves in a hazy hue,
Clashing with leaves in brilliant yellow and orange tints.
I hug the moment and savor its passing
And sit quietly watching the leaves silently fall,
Forming yellow mottled patterns on the newly seeded lawn.
I lost myself in the moment and relished what was left of today.
Until the past fades and the trivial is no longer important,
I climb into bed, free from expectations,
Already engulfed in the memories of yesterday.
Tomorrow another fall, another sunset will be here,
And the cycle of life will continue.
And so I slumber away with contentment,
Knowing that I have taken charge of today.

Franklin W. Douglas

Nothing remains static forever, not even one's thoughts and dreams. Everything evolves, expands, and modifies to create a more dynamic society. If you are not conscious of the evolution of time and space, just look at where you were then and where you are now. Only then you can see where you are going.

—Franklin W. Douglas

It is with this kind of thinking that Franklin W. Douglas's passion for writing poetry began. He was born in Beckford Kraal Clarendon, Jamaica. At some point thereafter a dyslexic pattern exploded inside him that could not be contained or cooped up any longer. We may call it "the expulsion of an inquisitive curiosity" that wanted to come out, to unleash, to explore, to strip naked and expose its virtues.

Two expatriate teachers impacted his secondary education during his tenure at the Edwin Allen High School. They brought his creative thinking, expressed in writing and analysis, to the fore. He took on writing poetry as an internal expression within dimensions, and it became the vessel for expression of his thoughts. Ever since starting in this genre, he remains on an explosive continuum, as he can see a horizon beyond the horizon that leads to infinitely more horizons.

Franklin is a lifelong learner, always acquiring knowledge. His studies led him from the Jamaican School of Agriculture to Tuskegee University in Tuskegee, Alabama, where he earned a bachelor's degree in animal science. He was awarded a Canadian Commonwealth

Scholarship to the University of Guelph in Ontario, Canada, and earned a master of science degree in animal genetics.

His studies, which were more scientifically based, did not stifle his creative writing skills. He chronicled a number of events, social issues, personal antidotes, and spiritual insights on the clarity of life and deaths that were happening around him, some in poetic form.

Franklin's poetry is vivid, vibrant, and philosophical, yet his poems resonate with all readers, especially those who are on the conscious journey of life. His writing is holistic, and he is always making plans to educate the generations to come.

Franklin is multifaceted and talented. His hobbies include gardening, plant and animal breeding, and, of course, writing poetry. He lives in Manchester, Connecticut, with his wife. Their only daughter has made them grandparents.

Printed in the United States
By Bookmasters